Memories
&
Images

To Sister Barbara
strong warrior Sister,
Scholar and
advocate of BLACK
Liberation
Peace × Love

Useni
2-10-03

Books by Useni Eugene Perkins

Poetry

An Apology to My African Brother

Black is Beautiful

Midnight Blues in the Afternoon

Silhouette

The West Wall

We Have Been There Before: A Poetic Narrative
Through Black History

Sociology

Explosion of Chicago's Black Street Gangs,
    1900 to the Present

Harvesting New Generations:
    The Positive Development of Black Youth

Home is a Dirty Street:
    The Social Oppression of Black Children

Children's

Afrocentric Self Inventory and Discovery Workbook
    for African American Youth

The Black Fairy and Other Plays

Hey Black Child: Poems for Black Children

Memories & Images

SELECTED POEMS

Useni Eugene Perkins

THIRD WORLD PRESS
Chicago

Third World Press
Publishers since 1967
Chicago

First Edition
Printed in the United States of America
Printed by R. R. Donnelley

07 06 05 04 03 02 5 4 3 2 1
Cover design by Denise Borel Billups
Cover art courtesy of Useni E. Perkins

ISBN: 0-88378-244-8
Library of Congress Catalog Card Number: 2002112835

The poems included in this collection were originally published in the following books: *An Apology to My African Brother* published by Adams Press, 1965; *Black is Beautiful* published by Free Black Press, 1968; *Silhouette* published by Free Black Press, 1970; and *Midnight Blues in the Afternoon* published by Inesu Productions, 1984.

This book is dedicated to the memories
of Ruwa Chiri, Sidmonde Wimberli, Cynthia
Zubena Conley, Conrad Kent Rivers, Langston
Hughes and Gwendolyn Brooks. All have been
an inspiration to me and have made an
indelible impression on my life.

CONTENTS

Silhouette

Midnight Blues in the Afternoon

PREFACE

I feel truly blessed and extremely grateful to Third World Press for publishing this collection of poems on my 70th birthday. I realize that all birthdays are special; however, for Black men the attainment of 70 should be a milestone to savor and cherish.

Poetry has always been my first love, although in recent years I have concentrated on playwriting and non-fiction. However, I believe poetry is the most challenging of all the literary forms because it demands constant retuning and refinement. The poems in this collection were written between 1965 and 1984. Many of the poems were written during the turbulent sixties when, like many Black poets, I was inspired by the Black Arts Movement. These Black poets, my self included, felt that Black poetry should raise the consciousness of Black people to stand firm against the tyranny of racial strife and injustice. In this regard, most of these poems are fundamentally political in scope; yet I hope they convey some insight about the human condition.

I am especially thankful to Gwendolyn Mitchell for sharing her editorial gift to help make this book possible. I would also like to thank both Denise Borel Billups for her graphics and Eloise Dotson for typing the original manuscript.

In the memory of Ramon Price, I would like to acknowledge his beautiful drawings which he allowed me to use to grace the covers of three of my poetry books.

I would like to thank my long-term brother in struggle, Haki R. Madhubuti, for his kind introduction. Finally, I would like to pay tribute to my father, Marion Perkins, who provided me with a role model that I can only try to emulate.

INTRODUCTION

I don't remember when or where I first met Useni Eugene
Perkins. It seems that he, his work and his energy have
always been in my life. I've known and appreciated his poet-
ry from the sixties, discovered his children's plays in the
early seventies and, in 1975, became his publisher when he
penned *Home is A Dirty Street*—now a classic in social
commentary. His work with young people is widely recog-
nized and respected, from his days with Chicago's Better
Boys Foundation to his leadership of the Portland Urban
League and beyond. He has traveled a long and honorable
road and now, at the beginning of his seventh decade, he
shares with us the main ingredients of his heart, his poetry
in *Memories and Images, Selected Poems*.

What does one say about a committed poet/artist? How
does one honestly approach the strength, weakness, vision
and life's work of a man who has crafted some of the finest
poetry of his generation, yet who is largely unknown outside
of his community? The question of where to place Useni
Eugene Perkins and his work in this unfair "business" of
poetry writing, publishing and public notoriety is a delicate
one. However, unlike his great father—sculptor Marion
Perkins—who never received the recognition he deserved,
Useni the son is still with us and *Memories and Images
Selected Poems* is his most comprehensive comment avail-
able of his powers as one of the nation's preeminent poets.

The public and private work of this sociologist and com-
munity activist on behalf of young people has, in many ways,
been the fuel driving the poet in him. There is his magical
urgency that is well-deep and fire-hot. Of the Chicago writ-
ers to emerge out of the dynamic sixties, he is one of the few
who embraced the mission of cultural worker/artist/activist.

He is multitalented and highly disciplined. Useni Eugene Perkins is a cultural writer: most of his work has a moral, political or ethical message underpinning it. This in no way takes away from the entertainment and artistic value of his poetry. However, it does place him in the very small company of conscientious poets whose work is a testament to a whole heart encircled by a love that is undiminished by time, circumstance or current struggles.

This collection of poems displays a major mind at work. The significance of *Memories and Images* is that it makes it undeniably clear that Useni Eugene Perkins is vastly underrated as a poet. His voice is a fine-tuned trumpet articulating the passions, desires, hopes, struggles and visions of African people. His poetry is not that of the seasoned desk writer detached from reality, surrounded by books, pens, paper and a suffering self. His poetry is that of a well-schooled artist and a sensitive son. There is a learned and feeling mind working here; however, it is contexted within the rough texture and indomitable spirit of Black people. He has succeeded in the poet's work, giving us the inner callings of a complex, often confused, yet beautiful and magnificent people.

Memories and Images is a collage, a carefully woven quilt, connecting seldom heard stories of Black people captured in a world programmed against their development and confraternity. There is glorious music here. Perkins' poetry is influenced in a large degree by the only recognizable and original art form created in America: Black music. His tributes to Nina Simone, Miles Davis, Duke Ellington, Billie Holliday, LeadBelly, Roland Kirk and others are part of the answer to his artistic and intellectual evolution. Black musicians have always been ahead of their people culturally and it is apparent in this book that Perkins was nurtured early and often into the politics and songs of our first visionaries.

This should be no surprise. As the son of one of the world's finest visual artists he has good genes and lovingly pays homage to his father in the fine poem, "For Father:"

> *Untouched*
> *By revolution and sacrilege*
> *His spirit lives Conscious of humanity.*
> *And dedicated to a creative truth*
> *To which he sacrificed his flesh.*

Like most children of accomplished and artistic parents he was nurtured early in the cultural contributions of his people. This is uniquely clear in "Early Autobiography:"

> *it began*
> *in the early thirties*
> *after the rise and fall*
> *of the harlem renaissance*
> *and the incarceration of*
> *marcus garvey's dream*
> *when the sound*
> *of count basie made kansas*
> *city the citadel of jazz*
> *and mystical policy wheels*
> *rolled through black ghettos*
> *copping money from*
> > *(dead dreamers)*
> *i knew paul robeson's othello*
> *at 10 and heard the poetry of*
> *langston hughes paint black lyrics*
> *at 12   but still I*
> > *groped in ignorance*
> > *admiring the deeds of*
> > *washington/jefferson/franklin*
> > *and the back woods emancipator/*

However, it is the music that nourishes the formation of his mind and poetry. Throughout *Memories and Images* are poems declaring the significance of Black "classical" music most often referred to as jazz. His "Midnight Blues in the Afternoon" is an evocative and tender poem on the politics' economics and personal aspects of Black music that is all but ignored by the young, stolen by whites, but remembered in the hearts of elders and the musicians themselves. The "Death of Jazz" is a thoughtful reminder:

> they buried
> jelly roll morton
> without remembering
>   his name
>
> the horn
> of yardbird
> was sold at
> an auction
> to a music
> critic who thought
> paul whiteman
> invented jazz
> and lester's
> pork pie hat
> was crushed
> by the buttocks
> of an old
> spinster who
> patronized the
> metropolitan
>   opera

Perkins lovingly writes in "Baritone of Protest" of Paul Robeson and in "Jazz Poem" takes the reader on a journey of the early creators of this great music.

Useni Perkins is one of our finest contemporary poets whose voice is sharp, focused and unapologetically cultural.

There is an emphasis on community, individual responsibility and integrity, honesty and commitment. He is a narrative poet steeped in memory and deep love for his people and community. His syntax is highly personal, but assessable to most readers. His worldview is criticaily informed and should not be taken for granted. He is well aware of Black weakness and wisdom. He is cognizant of our impotence and strength. He has a poet's soul and heart and often they allow his themes to keep from running into each other.

He is profoundly respectful of his elders and teachers. His poems for Margaret Burroughs, Gwendolyn Brooks and Lerone Bennett accent his Chicago connection. His tributes to Martin Luther King Jr., W.E.B. DuBois and Robert Perkins are must reading for young people whose memories are as long and deep as the latest commercial selling shoes or bubble gum. Perkins writes in the tradition of Langston Hughes, Sterling Brown and Margaret Walker. He is anchored by the poetry that preceded him. This is evident in the depth and content of his best work.

The topography and style of his writing is in keeping with the scatting and riffs of our best musicians, as they communicated with music, he with words; Perkins juxtaposes language, spacing, lines and punctuation. His rhythms are consistent with his sensitive ear as in "Black Poetry is"

> black poems from black poets/memphis st. blues/
> lil green/wooden washboards/the middle passage/
> muddy waters/souls of black folks/parker's
>   lament/black poets with naturals/
>   chuck berry/moans and groans/harlem/
>   hot corn bread/john carlos running
>   an 8 flat 100/left over chittlins/
> be bop/be bop/lady day/a garden of negritude/
> leadbelly's guitar/pinto beans/nile river/
> mississippi mud/coon music/brer rabbit tales/
>   poems with teeth/

shining black prince/
black poets in old clothes/
spirituality of coltrane/

Poetry writing is a difficult and precarious vocation. Within Black culture and indeed American culture the readers and buyers of poetry are few, but strong and committed as young lovers drinking rain water in a hurricane. Yet, it is in poetry that true seekers are able to find their voices, fine tune their souls, reconstruct melody and memory and prepare for volcanoes and/or love. The poets are often alone, misunderstood warriors crying against a sugar filled and smoked drenched world and the only herb that keeps them going is an "indomitable spirit" as affirmed by this poet,

you came to us
committed in principle and deed
void of the stilted rhetoric
some men use to illuminate their presence
for self-gratification
you possess a gentle soul
and compassionate heart
that penetrates the shallowness
of contrived ideologies
soaked in yesterday's tears

One could easily end here with the truth of Useni Eugene Perkins singing in our ears but I would be terribly remiss if I didn't point out that he also runs a mean marathon and plays a half-way decent game of tennis. All is not lost with a poet who is poetic as well as physical in his delicate deliberations in this, the elder hours of his years.

Haki R. Madhubuti
Poet

AN
Apology
TO MY
African
BROTHER

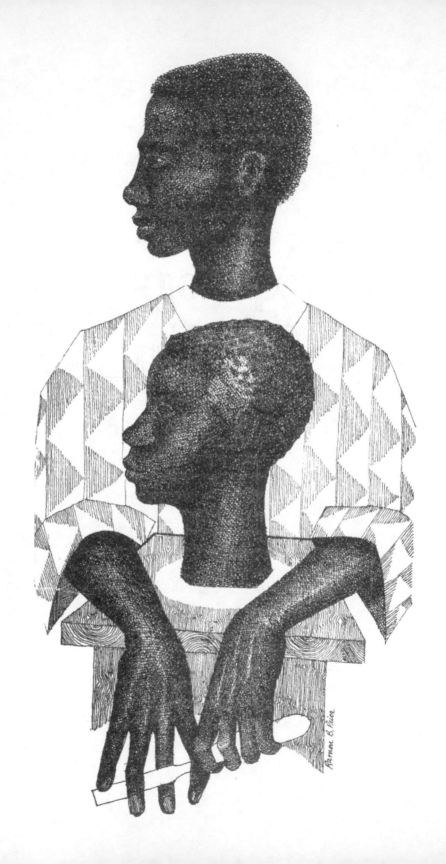

An Apology to my African Brother

Forgive me!
I have not been a faithful brother.
Memories of my heritage
Have been darkened by a cumulus sky.
My mind washed pure
To worship an albino God.

Forgive me!
Help me repudiate the years of apathy
Which branded me a Prodigal son.
Help my flesh to understand
Why your history was distorted
And the greatness of your culture
Damned of its rightful birth.

I rejoiced when you won independence in Ghana;
But like a coward I didn't support your struggle
My weary heart sickened with grief
When I heard of the atrocities in Johannesburg.
But I failed to be present at the burial.
Of your butchered women and children.
My admiration of your majestic art
Has remained but a pretentious facade;
For in my urbane apartment hangs
A reproduction of the Mona Lisa
And a painting by Grandma Moses.

Your scholars come to America
Enriched with traditions which have endured
Decades of wars, rapes and Christianity.
They scoff at me with disdain
For they know I'm benighted to my ancestry.
I've seen pictures of your primitive existence
Depicting ugly women with flabby breasts

3

And naked men dancing with poisonous spears.
I've read of your evil witch doctors
Who suck juice from herbs to heal the sick.
Bamboo huts, coconut trees and voodoo rites
They have symbolized your country.
But my eyes have been blinded
To the true beauties you possess.

O, if I could only build a bridge!
Over the sea which has diluted our blood.
And recapture some of the lost treasures
Long buried by European customs.
Help me black brother!

Our kinship must not die
As brothers we should not subsist
Castrated from common roots
An uprooted flower will only perish.
Forgive me!
I have been a fatuous child
Let me dance once again

On African soil.

THE GENESIS OF JAZZ

Abatutsi were your royal drums soaked in African soil
And sent to fester on the sidewalks of Charleston,
To hark the stentor of your tribunal ancestry
Where jazz nurtured in your amorous bosom?
To the beat of congo drums
To the beat of congo drums

Abatutsi did they castrate your copper hue flesh
From your verdant pastures of nobility,
And bring your crescendo to a hostile land
Of pliant cotton and blood smeared rivers?
To the beat of congo drums
To the beat of congo drums

I heard an ebony folk singer echo your chants
Along the umbrageous streets of New Orleans,
And saw you rebel against serfdom's tyranny
And search for concord in Mississippi waters.
To the beat of congo drums
To the beat of congo drums

Abatusi did you sow the pastoral seeds
Which King Oliver nourished in Kansas City,
And replanted in the clamorous belly of Harlem
Where Yardbird sounded his eccentric horn.
To the beat of congo drums
To the beat of congo drums

Abatutsi are you the Olympian of jazz heaven
Did your rhythms inspire the sensuous Lady Day
To sing the blues like a melancholy child
And make jazz dance in Louie Satchmo's trumpet?
To the beat of congo drums
To the beat of congo drums

WHO'LL SOUND THE REQUIEM
(In Memory of the Mississippi Summer Project Workers)

Who'll sound the requiem
Now that the rustic Mississippi horizon
Has stretched its malignant silhouette
Over the reposed bodies
Of Schwerner, Goodman and Chaney?
Now that the crust of the earth
Has divulged their flesh in wrath?

> O God
> could you not
> have spared them
> that fatal moment
> which strangled
> their existence,
> in the wake
> of this diabolic
> tragedy?

Who'll sound the requiem
Now that the seeds of summer's awakening
Have been contaminated by false prophets?
Now that the conscience of a nation
Has beared witness to racial insanity?
What monuments can be sculptured
Out of the scarlet magnolia clay
That personifies their quiescent bodies?

> Will justice
> condone more
> blasphemous acts
> to rape the earth
> of its fertility,
> and make humanity

a mere fragment
of the darkness
which shaped
our past?

Who'll sound the requiem
To give dignity to their sacrifice?

Their flesh must not suffer
For a casual commitment ...
To fade away with the passing

Of another summer.

BLUES FOR LEADBELLY

I heard the blues weeping
From a wooden cradle in a Louisiana shack,
And saw a twelve string guitar bury its head
Beneath a batch of flabby southern cotton.

I heard the blues crying
Behind the steel bars of Angola prison,
Pleading for a piece of Creole sunshine
To melt away the scum of ruby tainted clay.

I heard the blues singing
While the voice of a tall black troubadour,
Wandered through the murky Delta waters
To the soul of a twelve string guitar.

I heard the blues laughing
Along the seamy streets of Harlem,
Where barefooted children danced like fairies
Under the shadows of solitary tenements.

I heard the blues praying
A jocular New Orleans funeral hymn
And Leadbelly laid breathless
Gently holding his twelve string guitar.

ARTISTRY OF MILES DAVIS

A lilliputian prince
dressed in
Italian trousers,
with a voice
dry as
parched leaves.
And a horn
which echoes
through the
night
with disconcert
emotions.
Bitterness
and
beauty
defies each other.
Pleads for
understanding
like a
retarded child.

An Egyptian maestro
standing
against
the aurora
of a continental moon.
Blowing
a jazz chariot
to a fat
Dutchman
who idolizes Van Gogh,
adores black women,
worships Buddha,
and praises all things

artistic.

9

IMAGES OF HARLEM

A lonely drummer
throbbing
a cadence
against
the rooftops
of grotesque
tenements,
while a bearded saint
proclaims
an elegy
to the
blues
which
strangled
Charlie Parker.

A rebellious artist
sketching
a canvas
of a derelict
holding the
King James bible,
while a
minister bellows
from his
storefront church
about prostitutes
dressed in
holy robes.

A fatigued old man
pleading for
God
to console
his misery,
while a
mortician
looks on
with a
fiendish grin,
and prepares a
wooden casket
for a night
funeral.

In Memory of Du Bois

Push back the soil!
The Reaper has once again
Extirpated a Titan from our hearts.
His days are now eternal.
He who stood tall as pyramids
Even the rivers sung his deeds.
He who spoke with elegance
His words stirred the mountains.
His image gave dignity to black seeds.
He should not be buried
As if he were a deviant waif.
His body should be rested
Under a monument of ivory marble.
Keeper of justice
Advocator of freedom
Defender of truth
Push back the soil!
Du Bois has fallen asleep.
We must not disquiet his peace
Now he can be free.

DEATH OF MANOLETE

The village of Linares
Felt the verve of the noonday sun
Coughed its spirit on the Plaza de Toros.
And the crowd waited with panting stomachs
To see the intoxication of the corrida
Unfold its epilogue on the ocherous sand.
And when the trumpeter blared the paseo
The melancholy prince named Manolette
Stood stately as a sun-tanned pyramid
To face the hunger of Islero el toro.

    They came to see
    El Numero Uno endure
    another day of pain

The sun began to sear
Like the sea of Acheron.   And the crowd
Gaped with fervent eyes as the ivory stilettoes
Of Islero flashed past the master's capote.
But the brave matador met each deadly karma
With the passion of a Spanish nightingale.
And his feet froze to the earth
As if Satan didn't crave his flesh.

    They wanted Manolete
    to risk his life
    for Azael

Then the Puritanical sky
Became debauched with umbra. As the moment
Of truth smothered the phlegmatic fear.
(The corrida was no sanctuary for dastards)
And Manolete lunged his gleaming estoque
Into the ponderous skin of Islero.

And felled like steel upon the ground;
His groin screaming with bitter serum.

O Manolete!
Did they ask too
much of your flesh

What a pity
Christ died on a timbered cross
Death does not spare grandeur.
The tongues hushed like autumn leaves
As the corrida's dust engulfed the soul
Of man's exultation over beast.
And the prostrated wind kissed the tears
Which trickled from grief-stricken faces.
Twilight came. And the verve of the
Noonday sun reposed its posture
In a tomb of bloodless lilies.

The village of Linares
didn't sleep that night

MARTIN LUTHER KING, JR.

He lives today!
Spiritual as the Himalayan mountains
A courageous black clergyman;
Endowed with Autumn's dignity
Dedicated to humanity's suffering.
A man whose unyielding faith
Reaches beyond the visible horizon
To touch a socially disturbed world.

There is no conquest in violence.
Freedom doesn't blossom when
Summer's drought has saturated in blood.
It only decays from a languish thirst
To adulterate graves of voiceless men.
Our doctrine has found renaissance
In the image of Martin Luther King,
Who has toiled to preserve the truths
Which Moses sung to ancient Hebrews,
And Ghandi resurrected in India.

He lives today!
A charismatic force
To make men conscious of peace ...

FOR MY DAUGHTER, JULIA

Creation is a beautiful flower
When it blooms in June,
Bearing the neophyte softness
Of an Ethiopian princess.
A priceless gift of nature
To grace the city's backyards,
With her big enchanting eyes
And soft mischievous voice;
Bubbling with summer's laughter.
A precious pearl
To make dark days bright
And bless life with a new hope.
Yesterday's dream of freedom
Took on significance
I realized then
The tragedy of wars.

The face of a beautiful flower
Is worth more than all the stars
That sparkles in the distant heavens.

CHICAGO

A beating metropolis choking from the fumes
of overworked factories ...

Where people are dwarfed by rangy skyscrapers,
whose steel frames lean
against alabaster clouds.

Where noisy elevator trains churn their
screeching cylinders over the
pandemonium of honking traffic

Crowded sidewalks with fashionable stores
and smelly hamburger stands.

Sleek boulevards winding through artificial
pastoral settings ...

Alleys cluttered with broken beer bottles,
feces, and rusty soda pop caps.

Gothic face museums
archaic cathedrals
suspended bridges

and blinking neon lights ...

Chicago
Cabash of the wheat belt
Where the blues are held sacred

And little children play in sand boxes

building for the future.

FOR FATHER

The flesh that was his is gone
But we should not mourn
The passing of a great artist
He deserves more than sorrow.

His art will never perish
Under the face of an adulterated sun,
For like fertile soil
It will endure winter's frost
With dignity and acclamation.
His chisel has been rested
Somewhere in the poetic space.
Poets rejoice and sing him sonnets
He has left you gifts to praise.

The artistry endowed in his hands
No longer immortalizes the beauty
Of his proud ancestors
Whom he carved with compassion
Out of the dark Ethiopia sky.
But the strength which he symbolized
Continues to nourish the earth.
With an esthetic challenge
That defies the Reaper's vengeance.

Untouched
By revolution and sacrilege
His spirit lives
Conscious of humanity.
And dedicated to a creative truth
To which he sacrificed his flesh.

Black
IS
Beautiful

BLACK IS BEAUTIFUL
(For Russell Patrice, born December 6, 1967)

You came into the
world a black child
of nature. Innocent
and naked of the guilt
that has crushed man's
humanity. Your future
has already been charted
by a history that tried
to kill your heritage.
Black children must be strong
They are already beautiful.
I regret you couldn't
be born into a world
free from injustice
and void of social atrocities.
Even my love for you
is no substitute for
liberation. You must
learn to endure adversity
for it's unlikely the world
will be liberated from fear,
when you are old enough to
understand its meaning.
Tomorrow is unpredictable
but your flesh makes today
more tolerable. It gives
one a sense of commitment.
A feeling of creativity
to attack senescent traditions
and build Promethean institutions,

that will save Black children
from mad wars that leave them
crying at night without fathers.
Be proud of your blackness
For it is beautiful
Cherish it with pride
And if someday you must
defend it with your life.

I'VE KNOWN POETS
(For Langston Hughes)

I've known poets
I've known poets majestic as Mount Kilimanjaro
            that towers over Tanganyika soil.
My soul has become enriched with poetic blackness.
I've known poets who can sketch a picture
            of dirty Harlem children
            and make them appear
            like African violets.
Strong black poets
who can compose a Bronzeville symphony
            of a "dream deferred"
            with celestial lyrics
that have the compassion
of a mother's bosom.
I've known poets
who can paint the horizon for a new awakening
and rejuvenate black folklore
            black culture
            black history
Poets who walk the streets of black hamlets
echoing the melodious crescendo of
            black proletarians
            black shoe shine boys
            black musicians.
I've known poets
who can stir the minds of black people
to feel proud of ancient rivers
            Euphrates
            Congo
            Nile
Poets who can shake the foundation of the lilywhite
tradition and sing rejoicefully of black

       people playing blues on Rampart Street
I've known poets
Black Prophets of humanity
who can erect ebony pyramids of splendor
and plant seeds for a garden of Negritude
I've known poets majestic as Mount Kilimanjaro
       that towers over Tanganyika soil.
My soul has become enriched with poetic blackness
I've known poets
I've known Langston Hughes.

BLACK HERITAGE
(For Margaret Burroughs)

Black history
has never been
a fad with you.
You were praising
Mother Africa before
her name became a
popular excuse for
some people to admit
their blackness.
You are natural
in your beauty
Not pretentious like
the cocktail women
who identify with symbols
and fail to understand
their real significance.
In essence you are
                    Africa
Because you represent
those sacred qualities
which make her so
majestic and
beautiful.

CONFUSED IDENTITY
(To A Soul Brother Who Wears A
Natural But Still Thinks White)

It must feel great to identify with
your heritage and let your hair grow
like a bohemian poet.
Now you can walk proudly like an
African Watsuti and mock those "negroes"
who use greasy fatback to groom their
                                      kinky hair.
Yeah baby you represent the new breed
You can ad lib about Egyptian culture/
rap about Ethiopian civilization
                        pyramid of cheops/
                        terentus afer/
                        taharqa/
                        ra/
You can denounce ebony for using
copper skinned models with blond wigs
and listen to coltrane/shepp/dolphy/
play revolutionary jazz.
Yeah baby you are beautiful
Black and Beautiful
You wear black power buttons/
African buda/leather sandals/tiki/
and practice swahili to the exotic
rhythms of bongo drums.
Under your arms you carry the liberator/
muhammad speaks/black dialogue and
Malcolm's "Message To The Grass Roots."

Yeah Baby you are the new thing
a true soul brother
connessieur of black culture
advocator of black nationalism
You're an Afro-American
rejuvenated by negritude.
You're beautiful baby
Black and Beautiful
But sometimes I wonder what would happen
if tomorrow whitey gave you freedom ...
whose heritage would you emulate then ...

No Love Songs in South Africa

An indictment against South Africa)

There shall be no love songs
in South Africa this year.
For love emanates from the heart
and in Capetown there are no hearts of love.
Only malignant coronaries which transmit the
warped brains of racists to bleed upon the
tortured bodies of oppressed blacks.
There shall be no love songs
to lull minds of black children to
dream of beautiful fantasies or soft
harmonious nights.   The blood of black
patriots still covers the soil of
Johannesburg with yesterday's sadness.
No songs to comfort the poor who die
from malnutrition and are buried in
black graves without markers.

There shall be no love songs
in South Africa this year.
Only congo drums beating dirges
and the screams of black mothers
calling for their sons to
come home from the dead
smell of diamond mines.
No love songs
for a lonely black widow,
whose husband's heart beats in captivity
beneath the slimy white flesh of apartheid.

No love songs
They have all been murdered
Assassinated by bastards who will deny
a black man humanity but steal his
heart so inhumanity might live.
There shall be no love songs
in South Africa this year.
They must rest in silence until the drums
of black people are rammed down the throats
of their oppressors. To beat death music
for those who dare steal a black man's heart
so a racist can live to torment black children.

BLUES

Drums of Yoruba
West African bongos
Nigerian blacks chanting
And then the slave vessels.
Sinister ships of christianity
sailing the Tempestuous seas
with black cargoes of gold.
West Indies dance festivals
for white slave masters
with oversexed tongues.
Memphis
New Orleans
islands of Africa
where King Oliver made Satchmo a Prince and
bestowed nobility on Kid Ory's Jazz Band.
                          Charleston Woman
                          Charleston Woman
carrying juicy strawberries
to lamented Work Calls and
                          Street Cries.
Guitar Blues during a chant
Chanting, chanting through the Delta
backwoods, where black heads numb from
the hangman's noose are submerged in
the muddy swamps of Mississippi.
New Orleans Creoles clapping hands
While Dixieland bands bring joy to
                          dead brothers.
Leadbelly prison songs
pounding a tattoo on hard rocks.
And during a chant,
Chanting, chanting to Memphis, St. Louis
and the filthy black slums of Chicago.
Urban Blues singers with sweat oozing

from their black faces singing gutter
music for brothers with conked heads
Howling Wolf screaming like a mad animal
while James Brown does his Thing.
Chanting, chanting,
chanting to soul
and the Blues continue
a driving black force
to remember Otis Redding.

JAZZ POEM

Dead musicians are not jazz lovers
even those who were buried to the
> funeral marches of
> Rev. J.M. Gates
> When Charlie Christian
died he left his guitar to be envied
by classical faggots with Ph.D.
> certificates
White imitators tried to claim Ragtime
until Jelly Roll Morton put them in
> their graves.
The stride pianos of Jimmy Yancey and
Meade Lux Lewis kept the prohibition era
from becoming a complete drag.
And Benny Goodman advocates used to
> sneak into Mintons
> with propaganda about
> Walt Whiteman starting
a new jazz movement.
While the Bean and Sidney Betchet
took an exodus to France
> seeking Parisian wine
> And economic survival.
Fats Waller and
Fletcher Henderson were doomed
for frustration because they were black geniuses.
Jazz was a whore
until Duke dressed her up in a negligee of
> African velvet.
The Birth of the Cool
> Jeru/Budo/Venus de Milo
> and a saint named Miles

Jazz at the Philharmonic
                    battle of tenors/Jacquet/
                    Stitt and a little brown
                    Jug named Ammons.
God bless Count Basie
for preserving the blues.
Evolution continues even though Coltrane
                    is dead.
And a new wave of jazz lovers are buried.

AND NOTHING CAN WE CALL
OUR OWN BUT DEATH
(Shakespeare - King Richard)

We are like pawnbrokers
engaged in a contest of wits
bargaining for time; scheming to be
resurrected even before Autumn's
leaves cover our fragmented bodies.
Can we compromise our weaknesses to
preserve what we only visualize in
silly dreams? It's a cutthroat world;
bloody, sadistic, morbid and void
of humanity. Even the beauty of
little children is destroyed by
false monuments. Every day is an
adventure in deceit. Few men become
creators. They are too busy imitating
success stories of dead executives and
trying to memorize patriotic slogans
that will betray them in war. (I once
knew a believer who read the bible
each night the moon showed its full face.
He only finished the Book of Genesis before
he discovered he was an atheist. Had he
read Darwin's theory of evolution; he
might have lived a little longer)
Each man clings to something ...
religion, philosophy, astrology ...
to prepare himself for the unknown.
The search for truth stretches to
infinity. No man can walk that far,
And in the pandemonium of urban insanity
there is a perpetual struggle for identity.
The world is too big for little people.
Music is the only language everyone understands

Society is a conglomeration of fads. The
man who deviates from conformity is a traitor
(until he develops his own cult) History
plants the seeds for all concepts. That is
why new ideas are crucified at birth. All
habits are learned behavior ....

                    smoking marijuana
                    homosexuality
                    masturbation
                    incest
                    LSD

And non-violent men are taught to murder
                    their brothers
Choice is limited. Even in a so-called
free society. Children born in ghettos
have cheap funerals. Revolutionists are
self styled deities who become dictators
after they gain victory. Power in the
hands of a maniac is a threat only to
                    sane people.
Executions and lynchings both have a
common goal ... to exterminate life.
A poet who writes of a Black Christ
will not be blessed by the pope.
And life continues

                    continues, continues and
                    continues ...
Everything we possess becomes driftwood
And nothing can we call our own but death.

BARITONE OF PROTEST
(To Paul Robeson)

I was a child of darkness
when I first saw your
towering figure electrify
the Erlanger Theater in the
image of a Black Othello.
But somehow you were lost
Misplaced in a burning history
Forgotten in the bizzare
transition of an excruciated
society. And you were
ostracized by a ravenous
nation that wanted to
showcase your talents as an
effigy of American paternalism.
But human events have changed
since your days at Rutgers
and the New Deal era of FDR.
And your lusty baritone
that once stirred a world
is absent from the
revolutionary presence
that it prophesied.
For you were too early
Like rare wine seasoned
before its time.

TO MAKE A POET BLACK
(For Conrad Kent Rivers)

"yet do I marvel at this curious thing --
to make a poet black and bid him sing."
Countee Cullen

To make a poet black
is to make him a child of Africa,
wandering through the glorious past
of a land enriched with nobility;
singing psalms of beauty to make
black people conscious of their heritage.

To make a poet black
is to make him a disciple of
Paul Lawrence Dunbar, Countee Cullen
and Langston Hughes; singing psalms
of praise to make black people
conscious of their beauty.

To make a poet black
is to make him a Harlem Blues singer
wandering through the squalor of
black ghettos; singing psalms of
protest to make black people
conscious of their present.

To make a poet black
is to make him a protagonist of white america,
wandering through the unglorious streets
of a land torn by racial strife;
singing psalms of rebellion to make
black people conscious of their future.

To make a poet black
is to make him a creator of symphonies,
A composer of black lyrics which can
resound a triumphant encore for a new
black world that is waiting to be resurrected.

To make a poet black
is to endow him with blackness and cover him
with the cloak of humanity's suffering.
"Four Sheets to the Wind and a One Way
Ticket to France"
To make a poet black
is to name him Conrad Kent Rivers.

Silhouette

Black Poetry is

black poems from black poets/memphis st. blues/
lil green/wooden washboards/the middle passage/
muddy waters/souls of black folks/parker's
       lament/black poets with naturals/
       chuck berry/moans and groans/harlem/
       hot corn bread/john carlos running
an 8 flat 100/left over chittlins/
be bop/be bop/lady day/a garden of negritude/
leadbelly's guitar/pinto beans/nile river/
mississippi mud/coon music/brer rabbit tales/
           poems with teeth/
           shining black prince/
black poets in old clothes
spirituality of coltrane/
                 poems of respect/
bronzeville/ellington's a train/paul robeson

AFRICA/AFRICA/AFRICA/dusty du wop/stagolee/
poems that burn wigs/bessie smith/
cleopatra/b.b. king wailing/paul laurence
dunbar's lyrics/shinola/pharoah's music
candy yams/good poems for black people/
ethiopia/black magic/plantation spirituals/
       work songs/chants/
       street cries/ditties/

black poets who can't spell/hip music/
space solos/sweet peas/biscuits & molasses/
gouster trousers/signifying monkey/
big o burning nets/zoot suits/bronzeville/
is
real poems/real/real/real poems/poems that
smell/talk/see/create visions/make images/
poems that are war songs/
   a poem is a poem is a poem
   is a poem is a poem is a BLACK POEM
     watermelon man/
     true life styles/
third world/black art/jazz harmonies/
love/truth/courage/
is the total/complete/absolute/full/

expression/   of ourselves/

EARLY AUTOBIOGRAPHY

it began
in the early thirties
after the rise and fall
of the harlem renaissance
and the incarceration of
marcus garvey's dream
when the sound of
count basie made kansas
city the citadel of jazz
and mystical policy wheels
rolled through black ghettos
copping money from
                   (dead dreamers)
birth place was 36 & wabash
                where wright's
bigger thomas was carved out
of the noachian structures that
towered over the abortive streets
of chicago's bronzeville childhood was engulfed in
fleebags and fdr's new deal
                (sacks of decomposed
                potatoes/stale meat
                and summer vacations
                at wpa concentration camps)
i knew work at 8 each morning before selling
papers at my father's crude
newspaper stand   i had to remove
empty wine bottles and wipe away the vomit of some
                (derelict's
                last supper)
i knew paul robeson's othello
at 10 and heard the poetry of

langston hughes paint black
lyrics at 12   but still i
                  groped in ignorance
                  admiring the deeds of
                  washington/jefferson/franklin
                  and the back woods emancipator/
grammar school
was a pervesion in chauvinism
each morning we saluted the flag
        and pretended to be americans
in h.s.
i regurgitated each line of
the constitution and never once
challenged its validity
studied stuart mill's on liberty
without reading w.e.b. du bois'
                  SOULS OF BLACK FOLK
after the storm troopers
invaded poland i began to wonder
whether or not the pope and hitler
                  had made a deal
                  to exterminate
                  all jews
                  or why a rabbi would
                  buy a volkswagen/
                  and drink german beer
when the murderous
bombs felled on
hiroshima, i
witnessed a
death like joy
celebrate
charred bodies
                  (only wall street economists
                  and 4-F industrialists
                          were depressed)

after h.s.
i pimped at three colleges
            on athletic scholarships
            and still never had
            a course in black history
the early years
are always confusing
they seem to offer nothing
yet mean everything

GHETTO ASHES
(For James Johnson)

ghetto ashes
blowing through the streets
into the lives of young brothers
who see themselves as
old soldiers   left without
           medals or monuments
to be buried in
wooden crates
      MOANIN AND GROANIN
      MOANIN AND GROANIN

the little children
will not play at
the funeral
nor will they
weep
for tears do not bring mercy
or buy food for momma brown's eleven children
who'll never take piano lessons
ghettos seconds are precious
fail to see the sunset
become extinct before the hour
and the corner remains the same
poppa gus searching for dreams
        in tainted wine bottles/
        sister lucy hustiling the
jewish merchant/little bobby imitating
a dead idol/momma brown trying to
feed eleven mouths   (she does not
         count her own)
      MOANIN AND GROANIN
      MOANIN AND GROANIN

and each day calls an early
       morning sun/the blues
       singer reminds us that
life has not changed
change/change/change/

       MOANIN AND GROANIN
       MOANIN AND GROANIN
       MOANIN/MOANIN/
       GROANIN/GROANIN

and he sang the
blues in his sleep
before the ashes
smothered his body
with particles from
stenchy garbage cans
before mama brown realized
that she was not responsible
       for the cramps in
       her children's
       stomachs
before poppa gus
could confess that dreams
were only pain killers
before sister lucy opened
her womb to a jack-legged
       merchant/who made her
       pregnant under god's eyes
and before little bobby
learned that his idol
was a coward who
got his "rep"
       from beating old men
       with stale hearts
       MOANIN AND GROANIN
       MOANIN AND GROANIN

and the early
morning sun became dark
              his eyes looked
              for nothing
(not even sunshine)
each man rises   rise each day
sometimes/but young   despite
ghetto brothers   high death rates

THE HARLEM RENAISSANCE
(For the Poets Who Made it So)

Harlem
began to awaken
after Germany surrendered
and weary Black soldiers came
home with impressionistic ideas
of Paris and freedom.

Marcus Garvey
arrived from Jamaica
to nurture a dream
of African liberation.

Jass bands
from New Orleans
kept Lenox Ave cafes
crowded til morning
and white patrons
hid their Manhattan morals
outside the doors
of Mintons
          Carl Van Vechten
          tried to make
          Harlem his
          "Nigger Heaven"
             (And almost succeeded)
Alaine Locke
talked of the "New Negro"
and the "l'enfant terrible"   (Claude McKay)
wrote of black men
dying "noble death."
         While Countee Cullen
      gave Africa a "copper
      sun" and Harlem a

Black Christ
And the tragic beauty
of the Georgian
cane fields
came alive
as Jean Toomer
made them
into lyrics
The poets became the pulse of
Harlem's body
and poured
into her
veins

Melvin Tolson's Dark Symphony/
Sterling Brown's Sister Lou/

and along came
Langston (Hughes)
"the people's poet"
and Harlem
became a poem too.

But nothing
remains constant
and the Renaissance
finally died
like dry
October leaves.

And Harlem
went to sleep
and waited for a
new generation
of poets
to wake her up
again.

REMEMBER SHARPEVILLE, MARCH 21, 1960

(For Dennis Brutus, South African Poet)

REMEMBER SHARPEVILLE
REMEMBER SHARPEVILLE
There was no warning
only the violent
sound of dirges
piercing the
humid air,
at their solemn
unprotected faces,
which could not
hide from death.

They came to Sharpeville
without their passes.
Only with strong bodies
and the will to be free.

Volleys of bullets struck quickly
And the torn flesh of
children, women and men
smeared the ground
with pungent blood.

REMEMBER SHARPEVILLE
REMEMBER SHARPEVILLE
The stain of apartheid
must be obliterated
from Africa's bosom.

REMEMBER SHARPEVILLE
REMEMBER SHARPEVILLE
For it is a valiant
testimony to our
unyielding struggle
to be liberated black people

Big Bill Broonzy

Perhaps
one day
after the
world is
put back
together,
and political
systems
become
responsible
institutions;
someone will
find your
old records
and let
the new
generation
listen to
your
music.

THE BLUES SINGER

Troubadour
of soul
unpretentious
of the cool symbols
which create
the private man
unadulterated
by technology
and plastic
skyscrapers
Life style
innovator/
late morning
riser/
evening shouter/
a vocal historian
true to
real roots
and traditions

BOSS GUITAR
(For Wes Montgomery)

Charlie (Christian) died
even younger ... but you
knew about his legacy anyway.
It showed in your chords
those beautiful chords you played so well.
Chords that bounced around
like black women dancing
to African rhythms.
Chords that others tried
to imitate but became
frustrated from lack of
technique that comes from
plucking strings without a
                    pick.

They were still talking about
Django Reinhardt until you blew
on the scene. (then the memory
                    of the gypsy died
                    like everything else
                    that becomes numb from
                    too much pain)

You could do it all
inspire other musicians to
break sound barriers/
invent harmonies (that moved)
show what Duke meant when
he talked about swing/or feel
          like Lady Day when
          she sung the blues
          about those sad
          evenings she left
          in Harlem.

White people use to laugh
at black banjo players/and
praise Arthur Godfrey for
playing a ukelele.   but the string
                          has always been
                          our thing.

Remember those Blues players who
could make a twelve string guitar
play chords that weren't even on
                          the charts.

Beautiful chords like you played so well
Boss chords coming from a BOSS GUITAR
Charlie would've dug your style
you both had so much in common.
Fluent moves/drive/soul/and of
course these beautiful chords
you played so well.

A Poem for Jazz Lovers and People Who Hate Wars

Blow the minds
of neo colonial imperialists
with a side from one of BUDDY BOLDEN'S
excursions in rhythm. Let the NEW ORLEANS
BRASS BAND play dirges for the pentagon's
war lords. Change the national anthem into
a blues sermon accompanied with a solo by
FATS NARVARO. And let BESSIE SMITH moan
over the silent grave of the unknown soldier.
Place jazz organs in all churches so the people
can pray to real soul. Build monuments for the
DELTA BLUES SINGERS and a tomb
        for JELLY ROLL MORTON
that will ring chimes of joy during phoney peace
treaty talks
            Replace midnight bombing raids with
            jam sessions that will wail until
            the ruins of war torn cities have
            been rebuilt with humane housing.
Abolish the draft system
and let those who crave destruction
enlist as mercenaries in judas' army. Commission
COUNT BASIE to write a peace concerto/with reeds
and percussions blowing sounds from the aboriginal
bush land to the azure mouth of cape horn
            and the music of SUN RA soar
through orbit leaving vibrations of love on the
planets of jupiter, mars, mercury, uranus and venus.
Abandon the space program and begin building
                        survival schools to
                        save the next
                        generation.

Cease the armaments race and join the battle of
tenors with ILLINOIS JACQUET and SONNY STITT
blowing on a stage before a group of
                              army deserters.

SAVE OUR SOULS
SAVE THE JAZZ BANDS   that were left dragging
                              their music on ramparts st.
SAVE THE FUNKY BLUES MUSICIANS with beat up
          instruments who have been denied
       scholarships to downtown
       conservatories.

SAVE THE USA from becoming
a first class whore and
being the world's greatest
carrier of VD.
Let AMIRI BARAKA write a symphonic poem
to unite the THIRD WORLD and a requiem for
              gluttonous nations that
          feed on the lives of
          unarmed people
          and JAMES BROWN sing a blues hymn
          for the UN security council.

Appoint OLATUNJI as
ambassador to south africa
                    to lead a choir of
                    white racists in a
                    song of repentance

Let there be no more Armageddons to
honor men with medals for being
hired assassins

(custer's cracked skull
can never be memorialized
under the
stained bugle
calls of death)

Ban the battle hymn of the republic
from being sung in nursery schools
and close down factories that make
atrocious weapons to
commit genocidal acts
under the name of   /god/

Let the world be a be bop serenade
a crazy chord/   an intermission riff
without a final chorus
RIFFING/RIFFING/RIFFING/

SAVE JAZZ
DESTROY WAR   Make five star generals
take violin lessons from
STUFF SMITH
Let the world be a jazz melody
and
save it from self destruction.

WE MUST NOT FORGET THEM
(For the Soto Brothers)

We must not forget them
They who died with young hearts
drumming with the sound of a black summer
These two brothers
who saw their future shot down
by mercenaries who hide behind the
cloak of a corrupt justice
Slain on the concrete battlefield
Infants of the new revolution
While the city hall politicians
with their split level minds
talk about law and order
and a humanity they themselves
cannot see/hear/or feel
They were the new drummers
and the sound of their drums
will ring in the air

We must not forget them
These two brothers
Who were our future
Our reality
Our fertility
and our vision
The holy man is blind
and the young must lead
The mentality of our lives
must seek revolutionary solutions
To save other young brothers
from crucifixion of death
and the sacrilegious wars of
lunatics with bloody hands
From yesterday that

raped our mothers
Invented nigger prayers and
made genocide a legitimate
act of democracy

We must not forget them
These two righteous brothers
Who did not turn their backs
Believed in life and the
sanctity of its children
Who tried to correct the
path of death that makes
black children into corpses
before they are strong enough
to fulfill their destinies

We must not forget them
and the sacrifice that
made them men
They were the true builders
The new generation that
made old generations open
their eyes to see the real enemy
They were our hope
The seeds of a new awakening
Our legacy of today
and ultimate liberation
John Soto
Michael Soto,
Let them always be with us
Not only in our dreams
But in our reality
For they were the new drummers
and the hymn of their deeds
must never die

Do You Dig Brother

Do you dig brother
Do you dig dig dig
Do you dig brother
Do you dig dig dig
Do you dig brother a new world
     fertile with black concepts/
     celebrating the tombs of ancient
     warriors/and kingdoms which shine
     like night stars/praising blackness
     with ju ju spirits
     affirming truth
          dig dig dig
          dig dig dig
Do you dig softness/the skin of a black
sister/resting against your wounds/wounds
of battle and victory/beautiful black sisters
     helping brothers to
     build black nations

Do you dig brother
     a new vision/a humanity of love
     and lovers/ready to scalp heads and
     hear the comic's laughter
     bury niggers' nightmares
     under cathedrals with decayed traditions
          dig dig dig
          dig dig dig

Do you dig brother
     revolutionary sounds/screaming
     from the souls of COLTRANE's disciples/
     composing black symphonies for our

                    mothers/sisters/daughters/
                    natural as they are/can be
                    will be/must be/
                    naturally be/
Do you dig brother
                    a generation of black men/being men/
                    acting as men/fighting men/men who are
                    men/want to be men/to help give birth
                    to new men/who will be the sons
                                    of real men/
                                    dig dig dig
                                    dig dig dig

Do you dig brother
                    the spirit of PRINCE MALCOLM giving you direction/
                    a fulfillment of purpose/love for another
                    brother/negro brothers/colored brothers/
                    afro-american brothers/black
                    brothers/african brothers/third
                    world brothers/becoming real
                    brothers/to each other/for each
                    other/to save each other/
                                                dig dig dig
                                                dig dig dig

Do you dig brother
                    the voice of RAY CHARLES bursting into
                    a night song/screaming with love/and
                    tears/to make your heart cry out
                    YESTERDAY/and feel good
                                        so good/too good/
                                        be good/is good/

Do you dig brother
         the energy of your soul/transmitting
         blackness/and the blues/the energy given
         you by blackness/to transcend/transcend/
         counteract/attack/attack/attack/counteract/

Do you dig brother
         together/we as a nation
         a black nation/with songs
for our women
together/understanding/aware
         of the enemy who
         lurks in our minds

Do you dig brother
for if you don't you better dig
         your own black grave

HE WAS REVOLUTION
(For Fred Hampton, Chairman Illinois Black Panther Party
assassinated by "Pigs," December 4, 1969)

Some people only
dream of revolution
romanticize its history
and quote the words of
karl marx and mao tse tung
like parakeets
with sterile tongues
Poets write revolutionary poems
Musicians compose revolutionary music
Playwrights write revolutionary plays
Militants make revolutionary speeches
But only true
revolutionaries
are made of
the gut
and stuff
he personified
He was total revolution
The Battle
The Struggle
The Sweat
The Tears
The Pain
The Passion
The Agony
The Death
The past and the future
He was total revolution
The Drummer that sounded the charge
The Panther who climbed the mountain

The Soul that made it live
The Believer who gave it energy
He was revolution
and his total life
Embodied its . . . SPIRIT

MALCOLM X

He
was
more
than a
mere
symbol
or a
fragment
of reality
for
microscopic
truths
he
was
direction/
integrity/
a rare
experience/
and while
others
were silent
his voice
roared
like
African
thunder

THE GLADIATORS
OR THE NAME OF THE GAME IS
SANDLOT BASKETBALL

            the cinnamon sun
glittered faintly upon the
sweaty bodies of
Black Gladiators
wearing oily head rags/
stenchy undershirts/
and jagged trousers of
                    rainbow hues/
while hungry spectators
with bulging eyes filled
each inch of the asphalt
            arena
                    digging the ACTION/
                    ACTION/ACTION/
a clash is heard on
the wooden boards and
tense hands entangle in
battle/sending oodles of fiery
                    blood splattering in
                    all directions
a gold plated tooth
finds it apex in
a cracked cheekbone
and elbows of steel
grind into each other
like rivets smashing
stubborn concrete
                    WOW/WOW/WOW/
                    POW/POW/POW/

                              then a muscular hand
                              palms the ball
and swiftly hurls
it to a jitterbugging gladiator
                              GO BABY GO
                              GO/GO/GO

who
begins to weave
downcourt like an angry
alley cat
his ebony torso brushing
past outstretched arms
that lunge at him with
fierce claws
                              GO BABY GO
                              GO/GO/GO/
at midcourt still at full speed
he changes gears/whips the ball
                              between his legs and with
                              the dexterity of
                              a harlem   pool shark
threads a pass
through a mass of panting flesh
to a bugalooing gladiator
                              GO BABY GO
                              GO/GO/GO/

who veers
to the charity lane
feints to his left/fakes
                              a pass/and then twists
                              his rugged frame toward
                              the broken rim
leaving two opponents prostrated
                              BOOM/BOOM/BOOM/

and with the grace of an African Watusi
glides the ball cleanly
through the undisturbed net
the contest ends
and as the cinnamon sun
collapses on the noisy arena
the evening verve turns
into a tranquil moonlight
filled with friendly laughter

Jazz on a Hot Summer Night

Children sleep disrobed
Sunbathers lie on the Siberian sand.
Tenements creak
At the timbre of mellifluous music.
The candent air throbs frigidly
Like an African drummer
On a moonless night.

A frightened cat seeks asylum
While an artist paints a canvas
Of natives dancing in snow.

The hazy sky creeps unnoticed
Upon desolate streets.
The brooding pavement melts
To the passion of Sketches of Spain.

A siren sounds
To intrude on the melodic darkness
A helpless man lay groping
In a stream of torrid blood.

Nimble skyscrapers sway
The saxophone weeps
A child coughs
A mother awakens
The pulse of jazz
Has befallen a city
Filled with tenebrous omens.

THE FOREIGN TRAVELS OF PROFESSOR J.B. (NIGGER)

Took a flight to Europe
and spent a week in Paris
admiring the gay mademoiselles
fling their legs at the Moulin Rouge.

Went to London to see the change of
guards at Buckingham Palace
and traveled to Austria to
hear the Vienna Boys Choir.

Spent two days in Germany
gazing at the Rhine River
and stayed in a Roman hotel
consuming Italian wine and spaghetti.

Saw two matadors gored
at a corrida in Spain
and took skiing lessons in
Switzerland and went
bob sledding in Normandy.

Came back to Harlem
wearing Spanish leather
shoes/Italian knit sweater/
French Apache scarf/Swedish
raincoat/Edwardian suit/and
a custom tailored shirt from Budapest.

Someone asked him had he
been to Africa //
And he replied in a
sophisticated voice ...

"Africa ... Africa ...
I've left nothing there."

BRONZEVILLE POET
(For Gwendolyn Brooks)

The streets of Bronzeville
seem more beautiful
because you gave them honesty.
Made Philistine experiences
more than monotonous copy
for obituary columns.
Helped black children
realize that filth and
dilapidated houses aren't
the only world they have.
That blackness is more than
being able to recite black poetry
or wearing a voluminous natural.
You gave them fertile
soil from Africa to
scrub their faces.
Lifted their pregnable hearts
when racist institutions
branded their minds
with inferior images.
And the clumsy tongues of
button-down collar bureaucrats
told them that America
was the black man's salvation.
The streets of Bronzeville
seem more beautiful.
The blues at Pepper's Lounge
begin to take on
greater significance.
Muddy Waters becomes
a living legend and even
first graders admire Otis Redding.

The shadows under the "el" tracks
along 63rd still hold fond memories,
of glittering neon lights
and mellifluous music.
And when we listen carefully
the buried sounds of the Savoy
Ballroom can be heard over the clamor
of screeching jitneys and street-
corner sermons.
And though Michigan Ave. Has
lost its aristocracy,
a few buildings remain
that have survived "mecca's" fate.
And the dingy food shack
on 35th is not forgotten
amidst the neo technology
of industrialized war schools.
Its hickory aroma trickles to the corner
newsstand where two retired
postal workers see their dreams
absorbed by a dusty checker board.
And senile women with their
moth-eaten shopping bags,
searching for bargains at
the catholic salvage store
aren't to be damned for blasphemy.
And the new black poets
begin to talk about
creating something
revolutionary ...
black life styles/
and relevant dialogue/
They take a walk
through your Bronzeville
and begin to discover themselves.

See true images/the gut of life
silhouetted against the transparent
fabric of the black experience.
A Blues Singer greets them
and fiddles on his twelve string guitar,
while little Bronzeville children listen
and dance to your poetry.

GRADUATION 1946
(To My Classmates Who Blew It)

we waited in line
for nearly forty minutes
primping our adolescence
and adjusting the awkward gowns
that covered our rented tuxedos

the processional began
and we strutted proudly down the aisle
staring at our parents
as if they were strangers
after the stars spangle banner
we listed to patriotic speakers
all say the same thing —
that we were the future leaders
and how society depended upon us
to make it free and clean —

with diplomas in hand
we paraded out of the auditorium
feeling a sense of urgency
and commitment to justice
for we were destined to be
the new leaders and accepted this
responsibility with cocky assurance

but as I look back on our graduation
and view how screwed up things are today
I can't help but feel that we blew it

PARCHMAN, MISSISSIPPI
(For Robert Perkins)

on Sunday afternoon
the sun is scorching hot
in Parchman, Mississippi
and black men in dirty blue trousers
linger with relatives and friends
recapitulating their past week ordeals —
working from dawn to dusk
in red fields that stretch
for miles and bear the sweat
and blood of overworked muscles

of cold eggs served at night
and the taunts of drivers
armed with shotguns to
prevent men from violating
the cruel laws of enslavement

of the cold dungeon
called Alcatraz and the
bodies it has claimed

of the brutal killings
that become tradition
and the code of servitude
that strips them of manhood

at four o'clock
the sun still burns
in Parchman, Mississippi

and friends and relatives depart
with only vague impressions
of what they've heard

for only the inmates
really understand the
brutal injustices that lurk
behind the gates of Parchman, Mississippi

TREE OF KNOWLEDGE
(For Lerone Bennett)

At first glance
he appears like
a fragile tree,
sapped of its energy
trying to endure
new seasons.
Yet beneath his
ebony trunk
lies a fierce
determination
that defies
propaganda
and provokes
sterile traditions.

His roots are
planted in wisdom;
blossoming relevant knowledge
to clarify the aberrations
of our painful history.
Not just a scholar
but an Evergreen man;
a consistent exemplifier
of black excellency.

Those who touch his branches
are most fortunate,
for they too will
grow more strong.

DEATH OF JAZZ

they buried
jelly roll morton
without remembering
                    his name
the horn
of yardbird
was sold at
an auction
to a music
critic who thought
paul whiteman
invented jazz
and lester's
pork pie hat
was crushed
by the buttocks
of an old
spinster who
patronized the
metropolitan
                    opera
when leadbelly
died the obituary column
listed him as a vaudeville
performer
someone mentioned
fats narvaro and started
to do   an indian
                    dance
with old
tom tom drums
(is bud alive)   is tadd dead
who cares
even record collectors
have faint memories

OLD ROMANCES

old romances
seem inappropriate to the
new definitions of today;
yet they were often tender
and laced with affection
that brought out the little joy
which touched our lives.
and though our nights
were crowded with imperfections,
we could still enjoy
the glitter of
glittering stars
and feel the coolness
of Autumn evenings
blow from the lakefront
death was always with us
yet we embraced and
pretended it was
only meant for others.
and often we would invent dreams
knowing they were not
always compatible
with our circumstances
and only postponed our
responsibilities and
perpetuated the myth
that our hearts
were liberated
yet somehow our
romances made sense
to us then,
even if they seem,
not to fit into the
definitions of today.

Midnight Blues
IN THE
Afternoon

MIDNIGHT BLUES IN THE AFTERNOON

the old woman

          with the fat belly

sits in her

          rocking chair

knitting a pair
of tweed socks

          for a blues baby

humming on the legends
of jelly roll morton
without apologizing
for her granny's

          craze for the

crazy dixieland bands
with blond trombone players
who pretended to read music

          which was never written

or forgotten
by the chant of darkies
dragging their songs
in darky bags of

          cotton dust

and the newborn baby
will be told of w.c. handy's
biggest mistake

          (allowing the white world
          to de-humanize his music)

and today where she sits
the orchestra never stops
for life in the urban renaissance
is an endless chorus of
shouts and screams and blares
and rapid paces of feet keeping
in time with the quick
inventions of   ibm machines

the logic of all music
is misunderstood by most people
except those who give it form/

        and like dry honey

becomes sapped of sweetness
the old blues singers are dead/dying

        and their cat calls
      tell us to be common like the   earth
and while the goon critics
give stars   we become victims of

        a western plot

to lionize the beatles
and to make tom jones
the heir to b.b. king

           the ghetto is full

of old guitars and battered drums/and
dreams are left in dismal attics
to dissipate in darkness

blues for momma
blues for momma
big fat woman with the big be(hind)
making music out of life
looking at the world
trying to be something

        other than noise

the minister's bongo drums telling
us how   to dance/shake our hips

        to be hip

because it is hip
and the jive melancholy
pushes our hearts
and the afternoon blues

        become midnight

the instant revolution

betrays the young boys and girls

                        pushing behind time
                        that which is past
                        but still today

and the insidious motions
of the charleston
make no sense

                        to the youngsters

who bougaloo
through their misguided dreams
not knowing that bessie smith
was assassinated by white hate
and nat cole only sang popular songs

                        because the blues

were considered unpopular
vulgar versions of low-downs
sulking beneath sluggish clouds
drinking mountain-grown

                        moonshine/

and hip strutters
are more than hip they are sometimes
hippies and the dusty du wops become fag music
those who die old
remember the savoy ballroom, beehive/
nob hill/mckie's and the vipers
where the screw
became a musical sanction
and erskine's "after hours" was never

                        played before midnight

and midnight became the
final note
of our mesmerized lives

ALL BLUES (gotta be somethin else)

Blue music
of the ghetto
begin to harmonize
the whimpers of
suffocating babies
street corner hustlers
and relocated sharecroppers
       hard times in the ghetto
       hard times in the ghetto
Rousing
sermonettes
hum from
battered store front
cathedrals that
offer salvation
for two bits/and
black men with
wretched faces
scheme to crucify
a (slum) Lord
       hard times in the ghetto
       hard times in the ghetto
A policeman's
shotgun explodes
and a black youth
soaks his face in blood
while a pregnant
mother on ADC
strangles a welfare worker
for calling her immoral
       hard times in the ghetto
       hard times in the ghetto

young boppers
lag pennies and
dig tight skirts
hug fat rotating hips
and white boys
with Chopin hair
search for Leadbelly's
twelve string guitar
All blues
singing of hard times
and death/bad luck and
no food/no jobs/no peace/
no nothing but blues
gotta be something better
to live for/to die in struggle
not only for blues/black
music for jiving about
hard times/hard liquor/hard women/
Bessie still belongs to us
but she's dead and her blues
are faded memories that can't
keep us alive/breathing
street blues/alley blues/
sidewalk blues/ghetto blues/
revolutionary blues/all blues
      hard times in the ghetto
      hard times in the ghetto
CIA gospel singers
in missionary dashikis
check out militants
with funky rap/rap blues/blues rap
all blues

and nothing else
but Big Bill's
recorded voice of
THAT OLD NUMBER OF MINE
     (ain't the same no more)
gotta be something else
everything in the ghetto
can't always be blues

Last Night Blues

Last night the blues came to bed
and hugged my soft pillow
With her terra cotta cheeks
Glowing like a passionate sunset.

I felt
her pulse
beat
like a
nocturnal drummer
and her
torchy lips
composed
a Harlem symphony
blue and sentimental.

I caressed her nymph-like body
And heard a trumpet cry and cry.
Until the night became tranquil
And the strings in her hair
Danced like a gypsy guitar.

And
the blues
hung her
dress
on a
lamppost,
as night
encroached
upon her
privacy.

JAZZ SOUL OF RAY CHARLES

Soul is the blues
crying from a wooden cradle
in an East Harlem tenement,
while an old folksinger plays
a melancholy lullaby to the
legendary crescendo of Huddie Leadbelly.
Souls is ancient Egypt
with its proud pyramids standing
on a sunburnt desert,
while the sweat from black bodies
pours into the Nile River
that flows through the veins of
                                        Africa
Soul is the beauty
of a black woman giving birth
to an Ethiopian princess,
while an African drummer
sends messages to the sun
blessing the child with blackness.
Soul is the naked pain
a black man suffers when he has
been denied the manhood of his
                                    mother's womb.

Soul is Bessie Smith
shouting the blues
in a jim crow hospital
and Big Bill Broonzy
dying a thousand deaths,
while the kid from Red Bank
plays a blues chord
with one black finger.
Soul is black
Genius even blacker
and the jazz soul of
Ray Charles is pure black genius.

LADY DAY

       she asked for
no personal mementoes
to tell her story
and didn't apologize
for her
unguarded life
       her voice
became the
essence of
our existence
       soft
       deep
the transmitter
of our most
basic life style
       not always
what we wanted
but what life gave us

the core of our reality
she turned it into music
and made some of us
       sad
and others
       happy
but left
no one
with neutral
feelings

BLACK SISTER OF SONG
(For Nina Simone)

I hear your voice
a deep throbbing
of blackness
beating like
the staccato
of soft African music
a sensuous sound
awakens to infinity
and the rhapsody
you bring has the
       tenderness of
       black children
       playing games in
their dreams
and a piece of
soul/blues
blossoms from your lyrics
like a nightingale
nourishing its body
with fertile black soil
you are the melody
and the song
a euphonious symphony
of awareness and realization
a gift of blackness
is reflected in your voice
and the melancholy
of yesterday is
relieved by your
unquestionable
charm and beauty

THE MANY SOUNDS OF ROLAND KIRK

the music
was blasting
like a 16 piece
syncopated orchestra
in unity with
its soul
interplaying
creative rhythms
and revolutionary sounds
ala coltrane/shepp/dolphy/
and when
the music
stopped
Roland Kirk
picked up his
instruments
and neatly
packed them
away.

THE LAST FLIGHT
(For Coleman Hawkins)

The Hawk is grounded
his musical wings penned beneath
the earth
      BODY & SOUL
       still ringing
       with sounds
       from his
       last flight/
      Be bop beeeeeeeeeeeeeeeeeeeee
      Be bop beeeeeeeeeeeeeeeeeeeee
yet no more

flights/to
hark his tenor/
flights that
blew minds
of four
generations
      BLUE FLIGHTS WITH BEN WEBSTER
      DIXIELAND FLIGHTS WITH LOUIS SATCHMO
      SWING FLIGHTS WITH JOHNNY HODGES
      BE BOP FLIGHTS WITH CHARLIE PARKER
      COOL FLIGHTS WITH LESTER YOUNG
      REVOLUTIONARY FLIGHTS WITH ARCHIE SHEPP
      PHARAOH SANDERS/JOHN COLTRANE/

                  hot flights/
                  cold flights/
                  fast flights/
                  slow flights
                  day flights
                  night flights

flights that started in
st. louis/and landed in
harlem/flew over chicago/made
the west coast hip
to the east coast
    Be bop beeeeeeeeeeeeeeeeeeeeeeeee
    Be bop beeeeeeeeeeeeeeeeeeeeeeeee

flights that weren't even
    flights ... yet
    made TWA change its
    schedule to CP time
solo genius
    flight leader
    of tenor men

    legendary HAWK
who never spaced out
remained on the scene
kept an active horn
his eye on the future
    Be bop beeeeeeeeeeeeeeeeeeeeee
    Be bop beeeeeeeeeeeeeeeeeeeeee

helped young musicians
to play correct
notes without
being squares
taught older
musicians
that traditions
change too
showed them all
a vision/

and that the
most important
thing
was not
what you played
but how much

        BODY & SOUL

a cat could
put into his

       music

SATIN DOLL
(For Duke Ellington)

A Satin Doll
is not meant
for everyone
she is too precious
to be caressed
and fondled
by people who don't
appreciate the melody
of a rapturous song
or the sensuality
of sepia tones
coming from
muted trumpets
and saccharine clarinets

a Satin Doll
is for lovers
of mellifluous crescendo
who dream of
ebony-legged girls
swinging their
curvaceous hips
to the staccato
of a jazz symphony

a Satin Doll
is for dancers
who sleep
in empty ballrooms
after the band plays
the final chorus
of a Duke Ellington composition

BLUES FOR JUG
(For Gene Ammons)

religion and dope
have never mixed
except in the cracks
of crummy tenements
where cockroaches dance
even after being
seduced by rat poison
where the Deacons
were not church members
but gang bangers
and dudes with conked heads
stood on cluttered corners
harmonizing Nat Cole's
"Straighten Up And Fly Right"
in Black dialect
   Blues for Jug
   Blues for Jug
ministers and musicians
have much in common
they both excite audiences
with improvised sounds
and the jive hustler
will give odds
on a one legged horse
and the policy dealer
will cop nickles
from senile old women
   Blues for Jug
   Blues for Jug

during elections
the precinct captains
look for ghost voters

in the graves
of dead Republicans
and the mayor of Bronzeville
has no political clout
except to get tickets
to the Regal theater
but getting tickets
to the Regal theater
wasn't a bad deal
whenever Bronzeville's
favorite Jug
appeared on stage
        Blues for Jug
        Blues for Jug